gaia **organic** basics

compost

Charlie Ryrie

Gaia Books Ltd

CONTENTS

PREFACE

Soil Association

The membership charity campaigning for an organic Britain

The driving force behind the sustainability and environmental preservation derived through organic growing is the soil. The soil is the heart, feeding plants via an intricate balance of micro-organisms, processing organic matter to provide the range and quantity of nutrients required for healthy vigorous crop growth.

One of the most important ways to complete the nutrient cycle is through the use of compost. The composting process generates a material that plays an essential role in improving soil structure as well as 'feeding' the life in the soil.

The Soil Association has for over 50 years promoted the use of compost in optimising soil health for sustainable agriculture and we believe that this principle holds true from the largest farm down to the smallest garden.

This book gives gardeners an excellent insight into the importance of compost, covering practical considerations facing gardeners like what are the right materials to put into the compost and how can compost best be used to get great results.

Rob Hayward
Horticultural Development Officer
The Soil Association

Composting is an art as old as time, and it is as relevant in today's modern high-speed hi-tech world as it always has been.

Composting is the keystone of organic gardening. It is a sustainable practice, home composting being the most energy efficient and environmentally sound method of recycling household and garden green waste. And the end product, compost, is an effective soil improver which can be used all round the garden. Composted soil grows healthy plants.

It has often been said that compost is much more than the sum of its parts. Modern research is just beginning to discover the benefits that organic gardeners have always known. Compost can help to reduce soil-borne pests and diseases, and plants grown on composted soil may be less susceptible to pest and disease attack.

Time is limited for many people these days, but that need not preclude compost making. There are many different techniques for making compost; some are time consuming, others are not. Simply choose one that suits you and your situation, and get started. Your garden will never be the same again.

HDRA, the organic organisation, is one of the oldest environmental organisations. It researches, promotes and advises on organic cultivation for home gardeners everywhere. It works to continually improve composting, pest and disease control and other techniques, to enable organic gardeners to produce better crops of sturdy, healthy vegetables, fruits and ornamentals.

the organic organisation

An international membership organisation, researching and promoting organic horticulture and agriculture

Pauline Pears
Senior Horticulture Adviser
HDRA, the organic organisation

WHY

IS COMPOSTING SO GOOD?

Waste becomes wealth – everyone should recycle, and gardeners can recycle more than most. Anything that was once plant or animal matter can be composted and returned to the soil that originally nourished it, providing nutrition for new generations of both plants and animals.

WHY SHOULD I COMPOST?

Compost is a mixture of organic materials such as weeds, grass mowings, garden waste and kitchen scraps which decay into a dark crumbly mass, often called humus. It improves your soil, provides a balanced diet of nutrients for your soil and plants, it's easy to make, and it's free.

You don't have to have a large garden, you can compost kitchen scraps in a worm bin on a balcony if that's your situation; you can be a lazy composter or a manically enthusiastic one, you can follow strict rules or more or less make them up as you go along once you know how the process works. It's up to you – composting is not an exact science. There's a good deal of trial and error. It depends on your time and energy, the food that you eat and the plants that you grow.

When you add compost to your soil you add healthy soil life and help to control harmful bacteria and fungi, keeping soil and plants disease free.

There was a time when all gardeners composted, when waste had to be recycled because there was nothing else you could do with it. If you kept chickens or pigs vegetable scraps and garden waste were fed to the animals, their muck was then put in a heap, left to rot and spread on the garden to feed the plants. If you didn't keep animals anything that would rot was put in a pile and later distributed over the garden; other materials were burnt and the resulting ash was then put on the garden. Gardeners provided all the nutrition their garden needed from the home and garden. They didn't call themselves organic gardeners, they naturally looked after the soil and the planet, using available resources wisely.

Recycling material

Nowadays we don't have to recycle, we can choose to have our waste taken away to landfill sites. We don't have to think about the amount of waste we produce because we don't have to deal with it ourselves. Around 60 per cent of domestic waste is organic matter, and much of the other 40 per cent is packaging.

When you compost you not only reduce your waste output, lessening the problem of using tracts of land for waste disposal, at the same time you reduce the need to bring materials in from outside to enrich your garden. You won't need extra fertilisers or composts if you can make your own. One of the principles of organic gardening is to be as self-sufficient as possible in the materials you need, avoiding the use of energy on transport and processing. When you compost you fulfil this principle.

Recycling nutrition

Maintaining a healthy soil is the cornerstone of organic gardening. Get this right and everything else will follow. The way to do this is to keep feeding your soil by adding organic matter, and garden compost is the best material of all. When you recycle organic matter into your soil you are returning plants and tiny living creatures that once came from it, in the form of minerals, proteins, carbohydrates and sugars. These provide the nutrients plants and animals need to grow, then they in turn die, decay, and provide more food for future generations. So you are helping to maintain the cycle of fertility.

Helping nature

Whenever a plant or animal dies and falls to the ground it will eventually rot down and ultimately return to the soil. Leaves and twigs for example fall, rot and feed the tree above with nutrients that once came from the tree. So why don't we just leave vegetation to compost itself?

For one thing, few gardeners would like to have rotting bits of vegetation all round the place. More important is that organic matter is rotted by the action of tiny organisms, and if they come across a chunk of unrotted material in or on the soil they take nutrients from the soil to help them decompose it. So every time they have to get to work to rot something down into a form where it can be reintegrated into the soil, they are temporarily robbing the soil of elements that it needs to feed plants.

When the processes are confined to a compost heap they are altogether more efficient. Composting also mixes different materials so you end up with a wide spread of balanced elements, rather than concentration of a few, and the composted plant foods are stored and released slowly into the soil when they are needed.

Free food

The only mystery about composting is why everybody doesn't do it. Whatever your situation, if you want to improve your garden's health while saving energy and money, the raw materials for compost are everywhere around you, for free.

If you dig garden rubbish directly into the soil you can cause a reduction rather than increase in yield. Young and sappy stuff can be dug in because it breaks down fast but old stemmy materials will rob the soil of essential nitrogen as bacteria break it down.

If you don't make enough – buy it
If you don't generate enough waste materials to make as much compost as you need, buy more readymade. Many local councils sell recycled municipal waste, ranging from leafmould to manure. It may not have the wide range of nutrients that good homemade garden compost will contain, but suppliers will be able to tell you exactly what the compost contains so you can decide how best to use it.

WHAT

IS COMPOSTING ALL ABOUT?

It's very simple but it seems like magic. You throw all your kitchen and garden rubbish onto a heap, add a bit of muck and maybe one or two extras, and tiny creatures convert it into crumbly sweet smelling stuff that plants can feed from as and when they need it.

WHAT HAPPENS WHEN I COMPOST?

Micro-organisms in the compost heap need carbon (C), nitrogen (N), phosphorus (P) and potassium (K) to make the enzymes that transform matter into the humus that feeds plants. So a compost heap should contain a variety of materials.

Compost needs air so that aerobic bacteria can get to work. Most materials will eventually decay through anaerobic decomposition but this is more akin to putrefaction, where air is largely excluded. An anaerobic heap will smell unpleasant and resulting compost will be slimy and hard to integrate although it will break down eventually. Keep a heap aerated by mixing materials well or turning occasionally.

All organic matter contains carbohydrates and proteins. During composting carbohydrates (starches and sugars) break down to simple sugars, organic acids and carbon dioxide to be released in the soil. Proteins decompose into peptides and amino acids, then to available ammonium compounds and atmospheric nitrogen. Ammonium compounds are changed by nitrifying bacteria into nitrates – supplying soil nitrogen.

You don't have to get too technical about compost, as decomposition of organic material is a perfectly natural process that will eventually happen whatever you do, but the more you know about what goes on when you compost, the easier it is to get the best results. You may find the processes at work quite fascinating, as your compost heap is not just a pile of old waste but a teeming pile of life and energy: macro-organisms and micro-organisms, chemical processes and physical ones, reproduction, death, new life....it's a seething hotbed of activity.

Organisms at work

As soon as you lay down some organic material into a compost pile organisms get to work. All organic matter contains substances that plants need to grow, but these remain locked up until transformed by decomposing organisms into forms that plants can use.

Macro-organisms include mites, centipedes, millipedes, spiders, springtails, beetles, ants, flies, nematodes and earthworms. They start the work of decomposing, dragging materials through the heap, and chewing, grinding, sucking and tearing them into smaller pieces. The smaller the pieces, the larger the surface area for the micro-organisms – bacteria and fungi – to get at. These then digest whatever they come across, liberating nutritious elements locked into the waste.

Bacteria

The bacteria in compost heaps depend on the material, the temperature, moisture and air content. Bacteria produce enzymes to digest whatever organic material is available to them. The most important bacteria are psychrophiles, mesophiles and thermophiles. As they feed on the waste they break down compounds, grow and multiply and release heat as a by-product. The problem for bacteria is that they kill themselves off – as they work and reproduce they make their environment too hot to live, so they die or move to cooler areas at the edge of the heap.

Psychrophiles, or low temperature bacteria, start things off in colder situations. They operate at cool temperatures, below 15°C. As they consume fibrous matter they oxidise carbon and raise the heat of the heap so the next level of bacteria can get to work. In very cool areas psychrophiles will do most of the work so the composting process can take over a year.

Mesophilic bacteria are medium temperature operators, content (like humans) at between 15°C-40°C. If you start a compost pile in summer, mesophiles will get straight in there. In most compost piles mesophiles do the bulk of the bacterial work, but if they generate too much heat their job is finished. In hotter temperatures, over 40°C, thermophiles or high-temperature operators take over. They can take the temperature right up to 75°C. They are the shortest lived of all the composting bacteria as a heap shouldn't remain too hot for a long period.

Actinomycetes and fungi

Well-made compost has a characteristic earthy smell like newly turned soil, or freshly picked mushrooms. This is caused by actinomycetes at work. They are a higher form of bacteria that increase as decomposition gets underway. They liberate carbon, nitrogen, and ammonia from decomposing matter. Fungi also take over at the later stages of decomposition, breaking down complicated compounds and releasing further nutrients.

Continued benefits

All these organisms working together transform compost into nutritious humus, and as it is a living substance the beneficial micro-organisms continue their work of liberating and transforming elements when the compost is added to your soil.

It is not heat itself that breaks down organic matter. But the process of heating is created by specific bacteria that create the conditions for different strains of organisms to carry on the work of efficient decomposing.

In the right conditions thermophiles should be able to do all their highest temperature work at within a week. If a heap stays too hot for too long some vital elements can be damaged – for example, nitrogen will be given off as ammonia gas and the temperature will need to be lowered by turning the heap or aerating it in some way.

You can check to see how composting is coming along by looking for signs of actinomycetes – cobwebby structures around fibres in the heap. If these are plentiful you know the decomposing process is doing fine. As actinomycetes increase in a compost pile they produce antibiotics that inhibit bacterial growth.

WHAT DOES COMPOST DO TO MY SOIL?

Compost improves the ability of soil to retain appropriate levels of water. If plants have too much water they drown and rot; too little and they starve. Thirsty plants can't make efficient use of sunlight, so photosynthesis can't take place properly.

Plants grown in compost-rich soil can access all the air, moisture and nutrients they need.

When you add compost to your soil you increase fertility by improving the soil's structure and building it into the ideal condition to accept and use nutrients effectively. You also provide those nutrients.

Structure

In good garden soils the particles stick together in an assortment of large and small crumbs. But in light sandy soils large particles refuse to join together so air and water and nutrients drain away between them. While in heavy clay soils the particles are so tiny that they fuse together in sticky clods so air and water can't get through. Incorporating compost can correct both problems, lightening and aerating a heavy soil and making a light one more spongy and absorbent.

The water content is particularly crucial to soil. It should never be allowed either to get too wet or too dry, because plants can't get at the air, moisture or food they need, and soil life suffers with potentially harmful bacteria taking the place of beneficial ones. Compost soaks up water like a sponge – 100 pounds of humus can hold 195 pounds of water – then releases it slowly, so soil into which plenty of compost has been incorporated withstands drought, but should never become waterlogged.

Compost adds life to your soil, adding micro-organisms and larger creatures such as earthworms and insects that are nature's soil builders. The more life in your soil, the better the structure, and the higher the nutrient levels.

pH

Compost can buffer soils that are too acidic (low pH) or alkaline (high pH), reducing plants reliance on specific pH levels. Regular addition of compost may be all you need to neutralise a slightly alkaline soil, or you can gradually lower the pH by adding compost high in acid materials such as beech leaves or pine needles and wood shavings.

14

HOW COMPOST FEEDS THE SOIL

As plants grow they gather the minerals of their choice from the soil. When they are composted at the end of their life they return these materials to the soil to be dispersed.

Humic acids produced in composting can pull nutrients out of minerals already in the soil and make them available to plants.

The nutrients in compost are also needed by soil organisms which in turn provide plants with more nutrients.

The more varied the composting materials you use, the greater variety of nutrients your compost will contain.

Compost contains all the major elements – nitrogen (N), phosphorus (P), and potassium (K) – that plants need for optimum growth, as well as the necessary trace elements. It is also an important source of carbon dioxide for plant growth, as the organisms in compost give off carbon dioxide when they breathe.

The most fantastic thing about compost is that it releases nutrients gradually when plants most need them throughout the growing season. It works with the soil. When soil temperatures are low – when plants are young in spring and at early growth stages, or slowing down for the winter – compost releases nutrients slowly, but as soil temperatures heat up and plants move into a stage of rapid growth the micro-organisms in the compost and the soil work harder and release more plant food.

Micronutrients

Although micronutrients – iron, cobalt, manganese, boron, zinc, molybdenum and iodine – are needed by plants in minute quantities, they are still vital to plant growth and reproduction. Many soils may show signs of deficiencies, but high levels also harm plant growth. It is hard to feed the soil with a specific trace element in a form that plants can use without running the risk of building up excess levels and therefore potential toxicity, but compost contains and releases the elements when plants need them.

Almost all soils contain enough micronutrients, but they may be inaccessible. In very alkaline soils iron, copper, and manganese, for example, get locked up in insoluble compounds. But if there is enough compost in the soil the trace elements will remain available in solution. The other extreme can occur in acid soils, where you often find an excess of trace elements in solution, sometimes at levels which are toxic to plants. Compost is also able to mop up this excess and store extra elements away to be called on when needed.

WHAT MATERIALS CAN I COMPOST?

Coffee grounds and tea leaves are very high in nitrogen, also relatively high in phosphorus and potassium. Coffee grounds are slightly acidic.

Egg shells contain high levels of nitrogen and phosphorus and significant potassium.

Banana peel is high in phosphorus, potassium, calcium, magnesium and sulphur.

Citrus wastes are also very high in phosphorus and potassium.

Grass clippings are one of the main suppliers of nitrogen in a compost heap. Add them in thin layers, alternating with kitchen and garden waste and other bulky material to avoid them matting.

Seven pounds of hair contains as much nitrogen as 100 pounds of manure. Moisten it well and mix with aerating material in a compost pile.

Woollen waste and feathers are high in nitrogen. They need to be moistened well before adding to compost.

You can compost virtually anything that is animal or vegetable matter: if it lived once, it will recycle into nutrients for micro-organisms and plants. You don't need to worry too much about including all the plant nutrients in your compost pile. If you incorporate a good variety of materials, the necessary nutrients will be there.

Home compost

From the kitchen you can compost all food scraps apart from meat and fat. The smaller the pieces, the quicker they decompose, and you'll need to chop tough corn cobs, very woody vegetable scraps and old whole citrus fruits. Tea leaves and coffee grounds are excellent, as are eggshells and crushed seafood shells. If you cover or bury all cooked food scraps you won't run much risk of vermin visiting your heap. If this is a concern, don't compost cooked material.

Old flowers can be added, along with their water which can contain useful bacteria and moisten the heap. Old aquarium water is also a good addition to moisten the heap as it contains algae and other nutrients that can be recycled. Paper towels and napkins go into compost, along with cardboard tubes – tear them up a bit first. Newspapers will also compost but they should be shredded and soaked then mixed in well – don't leave them in a layer or they will compact, go slimy, and stop aerobic bacteria working.

Empty your dustpan and vacuum cleaner onto your compost heap. House dust is largely mites, hair and earth, all of which add to the nutrition in your heap. You can also add woodash, but fairly sparingly as it can make a compost heap too alkaline. Any natural fibre products can be composted, chopping large items up small. Feathers from pillows and mattresses, woollen and cotton clothing and even leather items will all compost successfully and add nutrition to your heap.

Most animal wastes can go into compost – poultry manure, rabbit or guinea pig bedding as well as muck from larger animals. But don't add dog or cat excrement unless you become an expert composter as these can carry diseases that will only be killed in an efficient hot heap. Human urine is a superb addition.

Just about any waste material from the garden should head for your compost. Weeds, soft prunings, mowings, leaves, even obnoxious perennial weeds such as couch grass and ground elder if they are dried first, and most weed seeds will be killed by composting. Chop or shred woody prunings. You can compost diseased stems and leaves as the organisms should be killed by proper composting, but if in doubt burn them, along with thorny and evergreen prunings, and compost the woodash.

Bringing in extra

If you are a keen gardener you probably won't be able to produce enough material from your home surroundings, but you may be able to get more from neighbours – people are usually happy to pass on their grass mowings and sometimes other material as well– or buy compost from your local council (see page 9).

A traditional rule of thumb is to make compost from three parts vegetable matter to one part animal. Animal waste keeps available nitrogen high in your heap, but if you have lots of grass mowings and leguminous waste you need less muck. Unless you keep poultry and several pets you will probably bring in extra manure. Strawy poultry muck is the best rich addition to compost, followed by cow, horse, pig and sheep. Never add wet muck as it delays decomposition. Always try and find manure mixed with straw because much of the benefit of muck comes from the urine content, but don't use sawdust litter as this takes ages to break down into useful nutrients because of the high carbon/nitrogen ratio (see page 27).

Woodash is high in potassium, but use sparingly in the garden as it is very alkaline. Keep woodash away from clay soils as it contains salts that can interfere with their structure and harm fertility.

Straw is good for bulk and aeration, but keep it wet and use in thin layers or it can slow composting by temporarily robbing the heap of nitrogen. Combine with manure for most efficient composting.

Leaves contain high levels of many minerals but little nitrogen; shred them and use in thin layers in a compost heap, but compost large quantities separately (see page 28).

Pine needles break down slowly into acidic compost, so add sparingly unless making compost for acid-loving plants.

Seaweed has more potassium than manure but less nitrogen and phosphorus. It contains most trace elements and is a valuable addition to compost.

Green bracken makes excellent bulk, and contains high levels of potassium and nitrogen, and significant phosphorus.

GROW YOUR OWN COMPOST

Phacelia tanacetifolia is an attractive living compost with blue insect-attractant flowers and feathery foliage. Use it as summer cover as part of a four-year rotation plan, or grow legumes such as red or yellow clover.

Winter tares are hardy winter legumes – sow them in September to stand all winter and dig them into the soil the following spring.

Sunflowers are easy to grow, quick to mature and shade out weeds in the process. Pick them for compost before they flower, before the stems get too thick and hard to chop for compost. Ideally gather plants less than 1.2m tall, as soon as the first buds show. Then just pull them up, knock off as much soil as possible and lay them in your compost heap with grass mowings and any other material.

The best comfrey for gardeners is a variety called Bocking 14, selected by the HDRA from varieties imported from Russia (see page 60). It is sometimes known as Russian comfrey.

If you get keen on composting, and want to import as little extra material as possible, grow some plants specially for your compost pile. Or include living compost in areas of your garden.

Living compost

Living compost – or green manure – is a crop that is grown specifically to be chopped down and turned into the soil. Legumes, members of the pea and bean family, are particular favourites because of their ability to collect nitrogen in their root nodules, so when they are returned to the soil they add high levels of vital nitrogen. Some grasses are also useful because they have spreading and penetrative root systems that help improve the structure of the soil.

Cut and compost

Sunflowers make excellent bulk for a compost heap, particularly worth growing if you have quantities of grass mowings to compost as the sunflowers add valuable bulk, aerate the heap and are extremely high in fibre to balance protein-rich grass mowings.

Marigolds (*Tagetes minuta*) are also worth growing for compost. While they grow they act as effective pest deterrents – particularly for soil pests such as eelworm – and also prevent weed growth because of the enzymes they produce. When you pull them for compost you add valuable bulk to your heap.

Comfrey is in a class of its own. Its strong roots can dig as deep as 2m to gather vital minerals which are made available to other plants when comfrey leaves are composted. It gets compost going (see page 23), is an important source of potassium for organic gardeners, and grows so quickly you can crop the leaves every six weeks or so. And sturdy perennial plants last many years.

COMPOST ACTIVATORS

A few handfuls of blood or bonemeal between compost layers speed up decomposition, but these may attract dogs and some rodents to cool heaps.

Once the organisms in your compost get to work you only need to provide regular supplies of varied materials for the processes to continue.

A compost activator kickstarts or speeds up the process of composting. It is a material that encourages biological activity in the heap. Activators such as young nettle plants increase the nitrogen and micro-nutrient content of the heap, providing extra food for micro-organisms. Others such as humus-rich garden soil introduce organisms that break down raw organic matter.

When you are starting a new compost heap it's a good idea to add an activator fairly near the bottom of the pile, then add more at regular intervals. Some people swear by a layer of compost from a recently finished heap, or a layer of good topsoil. Thin (5cm-10cm) layers of nitrogen-rich grass mowings are popular, or strawy muck from a poultry house.

Manure is a rich source of plant nutrients and bacteria, but always partially dry it first as very wet muck will slow down the initial composting process rather than getting it moving. Human urine is an excellent activator because it contains plenty of nitrogen and loses potency less quickly than most animal manures. If there's a baby in the house empty the potty on the heap regularly, and young boys rarely need encouragement to pee straight onto the heap.

Comfrey and seaweed are dynamic accumulators, which means they collect and store vast amounts of nutrients, and they decompose swiftly to activate your compost. Horsetail also helps speed composting activity – either chop it up (don't add the roots) or leave the hollow stalks to rot slowly, so adding aeration to your heap.

Make regular supplies of comfrey, nettle or horsetail tea by steeping leaves for two or three weeks in a bucket or drum of water.

WHAT DOES COMPOST NEED?

Commercial tumbler bins are designed for easy turning and aeration, and can produce finished compost in less than a month (see page 52).

All composting methods are designed to meet the needs of the organisms and microorganisms that decompose organic matter. They need a varied diet which is balanced in protein and fibre – nitrogen and carbon – and they need air, moisture and warmth.

Air

If there's insufficient air in your heap aerobic bacteria and soil organisms will die off, but there are plenty of ways to keep a compost heap well aerated. You can simply introduce air by turning your pile regularly, the more frequently you turn it, the quicker materials will break down. But this is not always practical, particularly in a sizeable heap, so you'll need to look at other methods.

Maximum aeration usually means fastest decomposition, so if you are at all impatient you'll need to keep helping your heap. You can place layers of pipes or thin poles at intervals through a heap and take them out as the compost gradually heats, or use organic matter for the same job. The soft centres of sunflower stalks rot away quickly to leave hollow tubes, so keep some stalks whole and layer them through the heap every 20cm or so. Jerusalem artichoke stalks do the same job.

Building air circulation

Some composters build off the ground, with wire mesh at the base, collecting any liquids that drip through and recycling them into the container, but it is much better to build a compost heap on the ground so that soil organisms can get straight in. In this case start with a layer of branches and twigs around 15 cm deep. This will be slower to decompose than softer materials above and will allow some air to circulate from below. Keep materials in the heap above fairly well shredded so the mass doesn't pack down too tightly and air can penetrate, and make sure you never add layers of over-wet or over-dry materials.

Moisture

Good compost should be slightly damp, like a wrung-out sponge. If the heap is too dry decomposition will be slow and the heap won't heat up. But if it's too wet air will be driven out of the heap, organisms won't be able to work, and you'll end up with an anaerobic smelly mess with most nutrients washed away.

The trick is not to add too much wet or dry material to your heap at any one time. Always leave very wet stuff like farmyard manure or fresh grass mowings to dry slightly before it goes on the heap, and mix any wet kitchen scraps well into the heap. Dry materials such as hay and straw should be chopped or shredded then watered well before you add them.

If your heap gets a bit wet you can mix in dry straw to take up the excess moisture – dried grass clippings are also absorbent. If it tends to dry out, moisten it with water (or urine which also speeds composting), or with compost, manure or leaf tea (see page 23).

Protect a heap from excessive rainwater by covering it. Polythene is fine as long as it doesn't touch the heap, and you could remove it every so often to be moistened by light rain. Cardboard or old carpet are fine if you don't mind their appearance. A thick covering layer of hay makes good insulation as well as a good water repellent. Don't leave your finished compost uncovered or nutrients can leach out in rainwater.

Warmth

Even cold temperature bacteria will be reluctant to get to work if temperatures drop below 13°C, so your heap needs to be well sited and reasonably insulated. Don't put it in an exposed area or where it is subject to crosswinds, and if in doubt you'll need to cover it well and insulate it with a straw bale surround or similar. Insulation will also help prevent the heap from drying out.

The size of your heap will determine how well it keeps its temperature. If it is too small the heat released by organisms will disappear quickly and it will never reach optimum temperatures; if it is too large it will take ages for you to get finished compost and the outer edges will stay cool. An ideal size for most home composting is at least 1m square. If a heap this size is properly built and insulated (see pages 34-43) bacteria should keep on working even in freezing weather as they will maintain the internal temperature.

Carbon/Nitrogen ratio

If you provide your composting organisms with plenty of material, air, water and warmth, you should have no problems. But you also need to keep an eye on the proportions of fibre to protein that you add.

Decomposers need carbon (from fibre) for energy, and nitrogen for protein. If there is too much nitrogen in the pile, then it is released as ammonia or other gases from the breakdown of the proteins in which it is stored. If there is too much carbon, it will take a population explosion of bacteria to decompose it, and they will use up available nitrogen for their own development, causing a shortage. They'll give it back eventually, when they die, but in the meantime nitrogen starvation means uneven decomposition. The same nitrogen starvation can also occur in the soil when you dig in living compost or fibrous mulches. Well-rotted matter is easily assimilated.

Garden and household waste will probably initially have an average carbon/nitrogen ratio of about 60:1 compared to the 10:1 of fertile soil. If the fibre seems to be breaking down very slowly, add materials with a lower C/N ratio to speed up the process; but if the materials reduce too fast add bulk with a higher ratio (see right).

Carbon/Nitrogen ratio	
Fresh sawdust	500:1
Old sawdust	200:1
Wheat straw	125:1
Oat straw	48:1
Bracken	48:1
Young weeds	30:1
Carrots	27:1
Beetroot tops	19:1
Seaweed	19:1
Rotted farmyard manure	14:1
Tomato leaves	12:1
Cabbage greens	12:1
Grass mowings	12:1
Good garden compost	10:1
Comfrey leaves	9.8:1
Dried blood	4:1

LEAFMOULD AND MUCK HEAPS

For faster results you can add 25 per cent volume of grass mowings to your leafmould piles after six months. Three or four months later you will have useable leafmould.

Well-rotted manure has the carbon/nitrogen ratio of good compost and can be used on its own as fertiliser or as compost activator.

Build a manure heap on ground that you later want to cultivate, as significant nutrients will leach from the manure into the ground as it rots.

Never use manure from intensive rearing systems, as animals are often fed with mineral supplements that can distort the balance of your compost. Never use manure mixed with sawdust as it is very high in carbon compared to nitrogen (see page 28).

Leaves

Although you can add autumn leaves to your compost heap for bulk, don't add too many at once because they contain almost no nitrogen and break down very slowly. It is best to rot them on their own into crumbly leafmould which releases nutrients very slowly, makes a superb mulch and soil conditioner, and can be used as a base for potting compost.

For a small quantity of leaves you can just scoop them, wet, into black polythene bags where they will rot down into useable leafmould. The decaying process doesn't need oxygen as it is carried out by fungi whose spores exist on all dead leaves. But if you have leaves in quantity, make leafmould in special purpose enclosures made of wire netting around sturdy poles up to 1.5m tall.

Rake leaves into the enclosures and when you have a sizeable pile wet and trample them to compact them, then add more. When your pile of leaves is up to the top of the wire, water the leaves further and forget about them for a year or so. If you have space you can leave the leafmould to develop for several years.

Manure

Manure is an important addition to the compost heap, but let most muck rot separately rather than reducing its bulk through composting.

Either leave small quantities to rot inside a black plastic sack, tied at the neck to keep air out, or make a manure heap. You don't want this to heat up too much or it gets invaded by 'fire-fang' fungus which destroys nutrients. So compact muck as much as possible to restrict air then cover the heap tightly with polythene. As the manure heats up and ferments steam will condense and drip back onto the manure to cool it down. The muck will be rotted ready for use within two to three months.

WHAT CAN I COMPOST ? – CHECKLIST

Get going
with swift to rot activators

Grass cuttings

Poultry manure

Comfrey leaves

Pigeon manure

Young weeds

Bat droppings

Nettle leaves and plants

Urine

Horsetail

Keep going
with regular supplies

Fruit and vegetable scraps

Eggshells, tea bags and coffee grounds

Vegetable plant remains – *even diseased plants can be composted if your heap heats up*

Well-rotted strawy manure

Straw and hay – *these are slow to rot*

Young hedge clippings and soft prunings

Hair and feathers

Shredded woolly jumpers and cotton socks

Hamster, guinea pig and rabbit bedding and droppings

Old plants

Old cut flowers – *purchased flowers can be very high in pesticide residues*

Vacuum/dustpan contents

Pond weed

Slow going
add in moderation

Corncobs – chop up well

Cabbage stems – chop well

Cardboard

Paper bags

Cardboard tubes and egg boxes

Woodash

Autumn leaves

Tough hedge clippings

Woody prunings

Sawdust

Wood shavings

Keep away
never compost

Meat and fish scraps

Fat and oil

Bones

Thorny prunings

Coal and coke ash

Blighted potato tubers or tomatoes *(stems are fine to compost)*

Dog and cat excrement

Disposable nappies

Glossy magazines

HOW

DO I GET STARTED?

Wherever you live, and whatever your situation, you can compost. Decide how much time you want to spend, how much waste you generate and how quickly you want results. Then choose the method for you.

HOW DO I CHOOSE THE BEST WAY?

There's nothing new about composting. Our most ancient ancestors probably did it without thinking and we know the Greeks and Romans had their own methods. Farmers the world over have always recycled animal and crop wastes. But the way we compost today depends as much on our personalities and lifestyles as on what our gardens need.

Hot composting
• *Advantages:*
Finished compost fast
Efficient use of space
Kills disease organisms
Kills weed seeds
• *Disdvantages:*
High maintenance
Balance of materials crucial
Need to add materials all at once

Cold composting
• *Advantages:*
Very low maintenance
Can add materials gradually
Contains wider range of organisms
• *Disdvantages:*
Takes ages
Doesn't kill weed seeds or diseases
Lumpy compost

A beginner should never take advice from a compost buff on the best composting method to choose. They will probably persuade you that theirs is the only way, while giving you the feeling that you haven't a hope of making good compost if you don't follow rather abstruse technical instructions. Nothing could be further from the truth.

There is a composting method to suit everyone. First you need to think about how much waste material you produce in your home and garden, how much space you have, how much compost you need, how much time you can give, and how organised you are – there's no point in setting yourself up to maintain a fairly complicated method if you have a haphazard approach to living or if you can only spend time in your garden sporadically.

Most gardeners will probably go for a cool heap, or even just bury waste materials. If you're very tidy you'll probably want a neat container. If you need to see quick results, or you like a technical challenge, you'll probably choose a hot composting method.

Don't be put off composting because you don't produce much waste – even one person's kitchen scraps can feed a worm bin to provide small quantities of highly nutritious plant food.

Hot or cold?
All compost is good for the garden but the varied methods of producing it offer different advantages to the gardener. The main difference between all composting techniques is the speed at which useable compost is produced. Hot heaps work very fast and efficiently, and can transform waste into useable compost inside two months. Some commercial bins have a tumbling mechanism to aid aeration and promise compost in two to four weeks. Cool composting methods take longer and are most suitable where you don't need too much compost, or where you have room to make several heaps.

There are also flipsides to each method: hot heaps can take a lot of work and although they destroy weed seeds and diseased material they heat up so much that disease-suppressing microbes are also destroyed in the process. This means when you use the compost it may not be as effective against diseases as that made by other methods. Hot heaps also need to be constructed all at once: you can't just put kitchen waste out as you generate it but have to store it while you build up enough materials to make an entire heap. And when the heap is constructed you have to keep a close eye on it and turn it every few days, which isn't practical for everyone. Hot composting is also less forgiving than cool – if the heap is too wet or too dry, or if the carbon/nitrogen ratio is out of balance you may have to make adjustments. However, you can safely compost even tough and diseased plant material, and the end result is very even-textured crumbly compost – fast.

Cool heaps don't guarantee to kill disease organisms, and tougher materials may have to be composted more than once. As weed seeds may survive the process the finished compost may be slightly weedy and tends to have a rather uneven texture, probably containing material at different stages of decay. But weeds are easily pulled out and semi-rotted lumps can be put back in the pile for another go. You can add materials gradually to a cool heap as you gather them, and as long as you keep an eye on the balance of materials to keep everything moist and reasonably aerated your heap should need virtually no maintenance. Also, the finished compost is likely to contain a wider range of living organisms than hot compost.

Some of you will prefer to compost in a container rather than constructing a heap. Commercial plastic bins tend to be quite costly and small capacity – usually too small for hot composting – but they are tidy and convenient. You can make effective containers that respond to your gardening needs (see pages 48-53).

Worm bins are ideal for small families and those living in apartments or with small gardens with no room for a bin or heap. A worm bin can produce useful quantities of compost from the kitchen scraps of two to four people.

Few gardeners produce enough compost for all their needs. For maximum production choose hot composting where you can produce up to six batches a year. You can also ask non-gardening neighbours to provide you with their organic waste materials.

WHERE DO I PUT MY COMPOST HEAP?

You can build a compost heap straight over an area that you are going to cultivate. When you remove the finished compost you leave an area rich in soil life and nutrients from the heap. Or you can spread the compost from the heap straight where it is needed.

While you probably won't want your compost heap to be the focus of your view from the house, gone are the days when it had to be hidden away. Other considerations are much more important. If most of your waste comes from the house and kitchen, you should put a cool compost pile somewhere easily accessible from the house. If you're constructing a hot heap this is less important as you'll need to gather bucketsful of material at one time rather than making regular trips. If the bulk of your waste comes from your garden, make sure your pile is somewhere with easy wheelbarrow access. If you're bringing in manure and other material from elsewhere, it's helpful if you can get a car somewhere near.

Sunshine or shade?

Don't site your heap where it is in a permanent draught or in deep shade or it will be hard to maintain its moisture and temperature. For the same reasons you don't want it in direct sun either. Ideally it should be protected on the north, east and west sides by some kind of wall or barrier, and open to the sun on the south.

Ground level or raised?

It is best to make a compost heap on the ground, so that earthworms and other organisms can get to work as soon as possible – this is another reason not to site your heap in deep shade where hungry tree roots will steal the plant foods and moisture. Evergreen hedges are also very greedy, so keep your heap away from them.

To increase aeration from below it is sensible to build your heap on brushwood (see page 24). Some people go for wooden pallets or wire mesh but if you create plenty of air channels through your heap you don't need to raise it off the ground, and composting can start quicker. Never build a compost heap on concrete or over plastic as this hampers aeration as well as keeping soil organisms away.

CONSTRUCTING A COOL HEAP

The earliest modern advocate of composting was Sir Albert Howard, who first experimented making compost to recycle waste agricultural materials in Indore, in India before the First World War. The 'Indore heap' is a cool heap of distinct layers, covered with a layer of earth.

Howard recommended building a heap with a 15cm layer of green matter, then a 5cm layer of manure, then a layer of earth, ground limestone and rock phosphate, then another layer of green material and so on. This is known as an Indore heap.

As long as you add varied material to your heap you can do away with extra mineral additions. However, it is sensible to add lime to the soil layers in your heap as the soil in most gardens in cool damp climates tends to get rather acidic when the lime is gradually washed out of the soil.

First decide what size you want. You should aim for a heap at least 1m wide, deep and tall. If it's any smaller it will have a hard time heating up at all and won't be able to retain warmth so decomposition will be painfully slow, or may stop altogether. It will also dry out quickly and may even freeze in a cold winter.

However, an over-large heap can be difficult to manage, and unless you are very careful air won't be able to reach the centre and material will tend to pack down unevenly. If you need to aerate by hand it's hard work trying to turn a heap that's much taller or wider than 1.5m. If you have a lot of material to compost it's much better to make several smaller heaps than one huge one.

Layering materials

Always try and lay down as large a volume of material as possible to start a compost heap – even though it's fine to add materials gradually as they're available, it's still best to add as much as you can in one go. It gives the organisms something to work with so they can get the whole process going, and so they don't starve.

A favourite composting formula is to start with a layer of branches and twigs, or build straight on the ground if you're confident of keeping the heap aerated. Then add a layer of grass mowings, or a layer of kitchen and garden waste that will rot down easily, followed by a dry layer of straw twigs or paper. Add a layer of muck and start again with grass. However, you are unlikely often to have materials in just this combination, so just try and layer your heap by alternating nitrogen-rich and fibre-rich layers, wetter with drier and so on. You won't need much – or any – muck if you add plenty of other nitrogen-rich materials.

You can include layers of particular materials to make compost for specific conditions (see page 18-19). Soil in most urban gardens is often slightly acid, so include a sprinkling of lime every few layers.

Easy compost

The purpose of layering is to create a reasonably controlled mixture of different types of organic matter. But it is easier for a lot of home composters just to mix as you go, particularly if much of your compost is household waste. Keep the pieces of waste small or chop them, and add garden waste, or moist straw, or a touch of manure or topsoil every so often. If you grow your own produce and eat well you will produce varied nutrient-rich waste from kitchen and garden and shouldn't need much else to make excellent compost. When your heap reaches the optimum size, cover it with a layer of earth and leave it for a few months before using it.

Composting grass mowings

The best place for grass mowings is on the grass, recycled into the lawn where they break down slowly to release their nitrogen back to feed the grass. The next best place is on the compost heap. It you recycle yours, ask a non-composting neighbour for theirs.

There's a lot of nonsense talked about composting with grass clippings. They are nitrogen-rich and perfect for your compost heap. You shouldn't use thick layers of wet grass clippings, or of any other material, because they'll stop the rot by excluding air. As long as you are sensible and never add layers of more than 10-15cm, grass clippings can be one of the most important nitrogen providers in a compost pile, reducing the need to bring in muck from elsewhere, and usually freely available from March to September. It's not a good idea to use fresh grass mowings that have been recently treated with weedkiller or hormone growth promoter straight away in a cool heap. Leave them to heat up and rot in a separate grass pile for two months, then you can add them to your compost or use them as mulch and they will still contain significant nitrogen.

BURIED COMPOST

Don't practise trench composting in heavy clay soil or you are likely to end up with a smelly slimy mass a few centimetres below the surface.

In hot countries pit composting is popular to keep moisture in and prevent heating from the sun. Compost heaps are built half underground and covered with soil or thick layers of leaves.

After backfilling a trench you'll end up with a slight surplus of topsoil. Put it to one side, covered, and use it in compost heaps or new beds.

One way of getting rid of your organic waste is to bury it in trenches. This is sometimes favoured by gardeners who dig the ground each year for planting vegetables, or before planting a permanent bed or feature, and is practical as long as you have reasonably light soil.

Dig a trench at least 30cm deep (45cm minimum if you are going to plant a hedge) and fill it with a mixture of organic materials. You don't need to be too fussy about proportions, but don't add very large chunks, try to avoid very wet or completely dry matter, and don't throw in too thick a mass of bulky material – if there is too much fibre bacteria will have to work very hard to multiply rapidly and transform it into humus, and will steal vital nitrogen from the soil in the process.

Mix everything well to try and ensure even decomposition, and top a trench with well-rotted manure or straw before backfilling with topsoil.

Disadvantages

It's a useful way of disposing of most kitchen scraps and some garden waste, but trench composting scarcely generates heat, so weeds will flourish and anything with a shoot will probably grow – a handful of sprouting potato pieces will end up as a line of deep rooted potatoes where you don't want them.

Don't grow root crops straight over a compost-filled trench for at least six months, when the waste will have rotted, or crops may pick up unwanted bacteria. Some people suggest trench composting between the planting rows of a vegetable patch, moving the rows over each year, but you need to be extremely well organised and it would be better to make conventional compost to spread as mulch, or fork it in gently – it's not helpful to tread on your soil more than necessary, it harms the structure. Trench composting is generally better as a one-off system rather than an annual routine.

HOT HEAPS

If in doubt, try and keep your heap three parts vegetable matter to one part animal waste. If you don't want to use any animal products in your garden substitute nitrogen-rich vegetable matter and extra minerals and compost activator for the animal matter.

Material should be packed loosely and make sure you chop or shred tougher bits and soak very dry stuff first.

If you want to make compost in a hurry you need to build a hot heap in one session. The best way to do this is to use a container (see pages 48-53) because the composting conditions need to be as constant as you can make them.

Hot heaps work best if you use relatively even amounts of different materials, and there must be a variety of tough and tender materials. Include kitchen and household waste, grass clippings, weeds and well-shredded prunings. Also have on hand some old straw or other bulky material, some manure and perhaps an additional compost activator (see page 22), as well as a small amount of earth with added lime if your garden soil is at all acid. If you don't generate very much waste you will need to collect it all up for a couple of weeks in buckets and boxes or open-ended plastic sacks.

Mixing, layering, turning

Whether you choose to start with layers or mix everything together is largely a matter of personal preference. If you do layer, keep a balance and follow a soft layer with a more fibrous one, or nitrogen-rich material with carbon-rich (as for cool layering page 39). Make sure there's a thin layer of soil every four or five layers, and include a compost activator. But a hot heap works just as well if everything is mixed before you start. Mix soft and stemmy materials, and make sure everything is slightly moist.

Fill the container to the edges and gently firm the contents down so you don't leave any large gaps which could dry out. Cover the top with old carpet or polythene, and leave it for two weeks. Then turn the material. Dig or tip everything out of the container, re-mix it, moisten it if necessary, and return it to the bin with the material that was at the edges now at the centre. The more often you do this, the quicker you'll have finished compost, but if all is well you need only turn a heap once every two or three weeks to get finished compost in under three months.

Problem solving

If you use a good variety of soft and tough materials, and watch temperature, air and moisture, you should get excellent compost every time. Beginners to composting should turn their pile as often as possible, because it's a good way of checking what's happening.

Sometimes the compost may break down rather unevenly, with some materials decomposing very slowly. They may be too large, in which case remove them to go through another pile, or chop them further or split them by bashing with a hammer. Or you may have too much fibre for the amount of sappy material and you'll need to mix in more high-nitrogen material. Slightly rotted grass mowings or poultry manure are ideal.

If you get slimy patches your heap may be too wet as well as airless – in which case aerobic bateria can't survive to work. You may have included too much dense moist material such as grass mowings in one go, or without mixing them in properly. Remix everything well and add stemmy fibrous materials such as sunflower stems or moist straw in layers through the heap.

Dry patches also mean a problem with aeration and moisture. Check the pile of materials and water any that are too dry before putting them back in the bin, packed down evenly. Cover the container with plastic to keep moisture in. If one side of the compost seems to dry out faster than the other, your container is probably not sited in the best place so you'll need to move it if practical, or insulate the more exposed side with straw bales.

Telltale smell

If your heap smells foul it is probably over wet and underaired. Turn it and add fibrous materials.

If it smells of ammonia it contains too much high-nitrogen material. Add fibre and turn it.

If the smell is sweet, the heap is damp but there's no heat. Add more nitrogen-rich material and turn it.

LET WORMS EAT YOUR SCRAPS

If you look in a pile of rotting manure or maturing compost you'll see dozens of small red worms with yellow bands. These are brandling or tiger worms (*Eisenia foetida*). They are the worms traditionally used as fishing bait and in composting systems.

Kitchen scraps are ideal worm bin fodder. The worms feed on the soft bits as they rot rather than chewing up the entire scraps. As they consume rotting material as it appears there should be no smell of rotten waste.

As long as your worm bin and the container where you collect the food scraps are well covered there should never be a problem with flies.

Worms compost waste by digesting it and converting the nutrients into a form plants can use. They excrete worm casts which are rich in humus and a fine crumby texture which is ideal for potting compost as well as soil enricher. Worm pee is also an extremely powerful fertiliser.

Most compost systems require a bit of space, or effort, or both, plus a reasonable amount of waste. But worm composting requires only room for a box, takes little time or effort, and the worms only need kitchen scraps which they recycle into very rich crumbly compost and liquid fertiliser. Worm bins are ideal for small families with urban gardens, even balconies or roof gardens. Keen recyclers who only have houseplants and windowboxes can use them because worm bins can even be kept indoors – as long as a bin is working properly it won't give off any offensive smells or attract bugs.

Worms' needs

Like conventional compost systems, worm bins need warmth, air and moisture. Worms have to have moist skin in order to breathe, they need air so the material doesn't get waterlogged and smelly, and they are most productive between 18-28°C so a bin needs to be well insulated if it lives outside in winter, and shaded in summer. The best times to start a worm bin are spring and summer when temperatures are ideal and worms are hungriest. Provide your worms with moist crumbly bedding and keep them in the dark. They also need a slightly alkaline environment so keep an eye on their diet (see page 47).

Unlike other compost systems, worms need feeding little and often, not much bulk – they are much more likely to die from overfeeding than from starvation. Worms will eat almost anything as long as it is chopped small, but concentrate on kitchen scraps – they won't destroy perennial weeds, weed seeds or diseased plant material.

WORM BINS

The more worms you have, the
quicker the composting, but it is
best to start with a small colony of
about a hundred worms until you
know you've got the conditions right.

Worms die in acid conditions. Their
ideal pH is around 7. Don't feed
them too much acid food, and add a
sprinkling of ground lime with their
food every few weeks.

Like other compost containers, a worm bin should keep moisture in and rain out, allow some air to circulate, and be able to maintain a fairly constant temperature. You can buy a custom-built plastic bin or wooden box complete with worms, but it is more economical and not difficult to recycle an old box or large drawer, or convert a plastic dustbin. Worms are freely available in muck heaps or from fishing tackle shops.

A worm bin doesn't need to be very tall, but choose a wide container rather than a narrow one as worms feed near the surface so the greater the surface area the more compost they'll produce.

Wooden or plastic

An ideal size wooden box is around 60cm square and 30cm tall. Never use chemically treated wood. Simply drill some holes in the base for drainage and line the box with a single layer of pebbles before adding worm bedding. Find or make a lid, which should have cracks for air.

If you convert a dustbin drill two lines of drainage holes about 10cm and 15cm from the base, and make ventilation holes in the lid, which should fit tightly for insulation and to stop flies. To keep humidity fill the bottom 10cm with pebbles and sand, and add water until it seeps from the drainage holes. Put the bedding on top of the pebbles – you may want to lay gauze first so the bedding and compost remains slightly separate from the stones.

There won't be much seepage from a wooden box so a newspaper underneath the box should be sufficient to stop puddles. But plastic bins will leak. Commercial bins are often fitted with a tap for siphoning off the liquid, which can be diluted 10:1 and used as liquid feed. Place a tray under a home-made bin and either drain it regularly to catch the more dilute liquid, or place a layer of compost on it and change it every two or three weeks, using the moistened compost on houseplants or in the garden.

Getting going

Mix up a bucketful of well-rotted compost, muck or leaf-mould (but not made from beech or oak leaves as this tends to be acidic) with some shredded newspaper. Moisten the mixture thoroughly then lay this bedding about 10cm deep over the pebbles, and your worm home is ready for occupation. You'll need at least 100 worms to start your colony. If you collect them from a compost heap bring a little of this material with them, otherwise just lay your worms in the centre of the bedding, and cover them with a couple of layers of moist newspaper.

Worms will eat any kitchen scraps but don't give them too much citrus fruit or acid food. Chop scraps finely – some people liquidise them but this isn't strictly necessary. Worms can eat any cooked remains, including meat and fish scraps, but can't eat very dry food.

Worms don't like too much food at once, so start with no more than 1 litre or 500 grams of finely shredded food spread on top of the bedding around 5cm deep. Don't cover the whole surface. You can partially bury food but then it's hard to tell when to add more, and worms are not deep feeders so some buried scraps may not get processed. Wait until the previous offerings have been well integrated before adding more. Keep the food moist and always cover it with moistened newspaper.

Extracting compost

You can remove compost a little at a time whenever you want, but if you want to wait for a binful – the speed depends how much food is added, how many worms you have, and the temperature – empty it in spring or summer so you can get your colony going again quickly. Remove the worms in a small amount of compost and leave them on one side, covered with moist newspaper, empty the bin, and put the worms back in to start again. If you have masses of worms, start two colonies.

Keeping healthy

If your bin starts to smell it means the worms aren't processing the food quickly enough. Reduce feeding – make a second bin if you have too many scraps – and check the moisture, temperature and pH of the compost.

If the contents of the bin get soggy check the drainage holes aren't blocked. Mix in shredded newspaper or coir to soak up excess moisture, and don't add extra liquid in the worm food.

Sometimes worms gather round the lid of the bin. If there are just a few this is nothing to worry about, but if they all seem to be trying to escape check pH, moisture, ventilation and temperature, and be careful about feeding. You can remove the worms, with a little compost, and cover them with moistened newspaper while you clear out the bin and start again.

WHICH COMPOST BINS ARE BEST?

If you buy new timber to make a
compost box, choose wood that
has not been treated with
chemical preservatives.

As long as you can keep it warm,
moist and aerated, and get at the
finished compost, any container will
do. Be inventive and make recycled
compost containers from old plastic
dustbins, discarded pallets or
disused building materials.

Compost can be made in any container that allows air to flow in and out, that can keep heat and moisture in and cold and rain out. Compost structures can be temporary or moveable, they can be beautiful and permanent. What you choose depends on your needs and personality as well as time, money and DIY skills. Inventive recyclers like to use cast-off dustbins, thrown-away pallets or dumped building materials. But you don't have to make your own to make good compost – effective plastic bins are also popular and widely available.

Simple one-bin systems suit most gardeners. Size is the most important factor. You can't easily make hot compost in anything less than a cubic metre, as you need a reasonable volume to maintain the temperature. On the other hand, an over-large pile can be difficult to keep moist, well aired and evenly warm.

Ease of access is another consideration. If you are turning your compost regularly you need to keep your container fairly low so you can scoop out the compost, or it needs to have a detachable front, or to be easily disassembled. If you can't get at your compost easily, there's not much incentive to look after it and you can end up with problems, so it is worth spending a bit of time and thought on your container.

Favourite boxes

Don't be put off making a bin because your DIY skills are marginal. Sectional boxes can be built by even fairly incompetent carpenters. Cut twenty 17cm-long blocks of 5cm x 5cm timber and make five separate squares by nailing 15cm x 1m boards to the blocks, leaving a stump on either side. Place the first square on the ground and fill it, then add the next and so on. There will be a gap of approximately 2cm between each section for air to circulate. Fill all five square sections and use a square of carpet as a lid. it is easy to lift off the sections to turn the heap.

Once a cool composting system gets going well you should be able to remove compost from the bottom of a pile while adding raw materials at the top. A bin with solid sides and removable slats at the front can permit continuous supply.

The 'New Zealand Box' is a traditional 1.25 m square wooden compost box. Boards slot into the front between two posts so it is easy to add materials and remove compost. Some gardeners use them for hot composting and build them with slatted sides to allow extra aeration. You could build one from offcuts or reclaimed timber salvaged from skips, or haulage pallets. Three pallets wired together make an ideal compost box – just stick a couple of stakes in front to slot boards into.

If you have a large garden and plenty of materials to compost you can have two or preferably three adjoining boxes, or make one large box in two or three sections. Fill one section at a time and leave it to mature slowly while you fill the next one, using the most mature compost. Or if you're very keen, with lots of waste, you can use three bins for quantities of compost, moving the heaps between the bins (see right).

Some tidy gardeners like to build permanent compost boxes out of bricks, breeze blocks, or even stone. If you do go for permanence, it's worth trying something else for a year just to make sure you have chosen the best site, and never make a permanent concrete base.

Insulation

They may not look neat, but straw bales make good compost surrounds, particularly in cool gardens where they provide insulation. The optimum size heap uses thirteen bales, stacked three high on three sides with overlapping ends. You can pull more across to close up the front, and cover the heap with a sheet of carpet or corrugated iron. Re-use the straw in future batches of compost.

Three-bin compost – fast

Make sure all materials are shredded, not too moist or dry, and watch the carbon/nitrogen ratio. You can get up to ten full bins of compost in one year using this method

- Week 1: Build a traditional layered hot heap in the centre bin, spread a layer of chopped leaves or straw in the adjoining holding bin and throw in kitchen and garden scraps daily.
- Weeks 3, 4, 5: Turn the centre heap. Keep adding daily to the holding pile.
- Week 6: Move the centre pile into the end bin. Move the holding pile into the centre bin, mixing all the materials well. Start a new pile in the original holding bin.
- Weeks 7 and 8: Turn the centre heap. Keep adding to the new holding pile. Turn the end heap.
- Week 9: Check the compost in the end bin. It should be ready to use in the garden.

Continue the cycle for a permanent supply of compost. It will take longer in winter, and if your supply dries up or tapers off for a while cover the maturing heaps with carpet or straw until things can speed up again.

CAGES AND METAL BINS

Any old iron?
Four sheets of corrugated iron, nailed to sturdy posts, makes an excellent container. Drill a few lines of holes in the sides to encourage aeration, and stand on bare ground, then add garden and kitchen scraps as you have them.

The compost in the photo (right) was made over eight months in a bin of scrap corrugated iron.

Stick four 1m-tall poles or stakes in the ground to make a 1m diameter circle or square, wrap wire mesh round them, and you have a mesh compost bin.

These bins are great for leafmould and can make adequate compost bins if you insulate them well by wrapping carpet around the outside or cardboard inside, and cover the top with thick carpet. Their pluses are economy, ease of construction and flexibility – join the mesh with wire clips and they can be dismantled in a trice so you can turn your compost or move the bin to start a new compost pile in another part of the garden. The main minus is the need for insulation, and you need to watch aeration carefully.

Dustbins and metal drums

An old metal dustbin can be transformed into a useful cool composting container. It is not large enough to make hot compost successfully unless you are prepared to turn the compost every few days, and even then success is not guaranteed. Drill holes in the sides, and a couple in the lid, for aeration, and site somewhere sheltered as the bin won't maintain heat effectively in cold weather. It is best if the bottom is pushed out so the bin stands straight onto soil and earthworms have easy access.

Old oil drums have slightly larger capacity to make more useful containers, but be very careful to clean them thoroughly. Take out the base and stand your drum on double rows of bricks on the ground. If possible drill holes in the sides as for a dustbin. If the metal is too hard insert a tube of coiled wire or a section of 10cm perforated pipe down the centre of the drum to aid aeration, and always start your pile with at least 15cm brushwood (see page 24). The central pipe should act as a natural chimney, pulling air up from beneath the heap. It is tricky to turn a metal drum, so build your compost in layers, inserting tubes for extra aeration(see page 24) and keep a close eye on the developing compost (see page 43).

PLASTIC BINS AND TUMBLERS

The main advantages of tumblers are speed and good heating, so weed seeds and diseases are killed. Tumblers are self-contained so there is no risk of attracting vermin, and they can be used where there is no bare earth to site a heap or conventional bin. However, tumblers can be heavy to turn, and will not produce good compost unless they are turned regularly to ensure aeration.

There is a wide variety of plastic compost containers on the market. Their volume is usually the limiting factor. Always purchase the biggest container you can – it needs to be over 250 litres for effective composting. Anything smaller will have problems keeping heat in. For the same reason try to find a container with reasonably thick walls and a tight-fitting lid. If it has a base, make sure it has some holes for drainage, but it shouldn't need ventilation holes in the walls if you mix the right materials. You need to take just as much care in siting and feeding a compost container as any compost heap or pile.

Containers shaped like inverted cones work well because any condensed moisture trickles down the sides, allowing the centre to heat up well without cooling, but keeping moisture in the pile. Square and barrel shaped containers are easy for access, for turning the compost or for removing it.

Some bins have removable sides for accessing finished compost, others have flaps or drawers at the base but these need to be substantial to have any value. It is usually more practical to remove the bin altogether, and remix uncomposted material to start a new batch.

Tumblers

Probably the most foolproof composting devices are compost tumblers, barrel shaped plastic containers mounted on an axle so you can turn the compost easily by tumbling the composter over. Daily turning means compost ingredients heat up well and keep well aerated for swift decomposition, so you can make finished compost in less than a month: fill the bin all at once if possible, mixing shredded ingredients together well, and when it is full turn it daily for two weeks. Then compost can be removed and the bin refilled. You can use this compost fresh on your garden but it is best if it is left to mature under cover for a month or so.

HOW SHOULD I USE MY COMPOST?

Compost is mature when it has largely stopped decomposing – when the main bacteria have done their jobs and died.

You can probably always find a use for compost. How and when you use it depends on what your garden needs, the characteristics of your soil, and on the state of the compost. The point of composting is to recycle fertility that has come from the soil, back into the soil, so using compost gives your garden a boost when it needs it, and promotes long-term health.

Mature compost should be dark brown, soft and crumbly. It may not be perfectly even textured, as some bits may not have decomposed as thoroughly as others, but this doesn't matter. You can pull them out or ignore them, depending on the compost's destination. Some gardeners say that slow composting produces the best compost, others swear by hot (see pages 34-35). The end results should be similar, but compost that has been made very quickly, as in a commercial tumbler, is best left to stabilise by leaving it covered for a month or so before use.

If your garden soil is light and sandy you can often use partially rotted compost, but if your soil is heavier you should only ever use very well-rotted organic matter.

Digging or leaving?

It is not a good idea to dig your soil too much. If you give it a thorough overhaul when you take over a garden or prepare new beds you shouldn't need to dig at all, unless you want to. Every time you tread on the soil you compact it a little, and digging can harm a fragile structure. This is why many gardeners use compost as a general fertility mulch instead of digging it in wholesale. As a rule, whenever you dig or turn the soil – to clear a patch of ground, to make planting holes for perennials, shrubs and trees, or trenches for vegetables – add a generous amount of compost as you backfill, otherwise leave it on the surface for worms and other soil organisms to drag down. You should then only need to scratch over the surface with a fork before further sowing or planting.

WHERE SHALL I USE MY COMPOST?

Routine management

Try to apply about 2 cm of well-rotted compost to your soil each year as a general soil fertiliser and conditioner. Use the compost as a mulch or fork it lightly into the soil in spring and summer. In established herbaceous beds, you can spread compost around plants in spring or autumn.

Storing compost

Compost made in a tumbler is best stored to mature for a few weeks before use, otherwise it is rare to have to store compost. Most compost is ready for use as soon as it has decomposed, although it will not pass on nutrients to plants for another couple of weeks when the soil microbes have got to work.

It is always better to use compost when it's available rather than store it for a long time because the nutrients within it can be leached out of a standing heap. Also, a long-standing compost heap can turn anaerobic if it gets too wet.

Always store compost on the earth, so any nutrients that do leach away go straight into the soil, and cover it with a thick layer of soil, or carpet or rotting straw. Use it within six months.

Planting

Before you plant, prepare your soil by adding compost to provide nutrients slowly when plants need them. If you have well-rotted compost lay a 5cm mulch over clay soil in autumn, and plant through that in spring.

You can leave a winter mulch of semi-rotted compost over sandy soils to break down over winter, and then fork it into the soil in the following spring. Or fork well-rotted compost lightly into sandy soil in spring about four weeks before planting.

Mix compost with topsoil whenever you plant a herbaceous perennial, shrub or tree. Mix the compost into the bottom of a trench before planting, for example, potatoes and celery. Potatoes can get scabby if the compost is not well-rotted.

Acid-loving plants appreciate slightly acid compost (see page 14), or add a layer of chopped leaves or semi-rotted pine needles with the compost when planting strawberries or acid-loving shrubs.

Sowing seeds
Fork compost into a seed bed, or incorporate overwintering compost mulch three or four weeks before sowing seeds. Be sure it is well rotted as unfinished compost can some-times retard seed germination.

No-dig mulching
Some gardeners choose never to dig their soil. Instead, they prefer to add 5-10cm layers of compost annually or bi-annually. All sowing and planting takes place through the compost.

Top dressing
Where perennial plants are growing in containers, you can rejuvenate the soil each autumn by scratching off the top few centimetres and then replacing it with fresh compost. Lawn-proud gardeners can use finely screened compost as a top dressing in autumn.

Liquid fertiliser
Compost tea (see page 23) makes an excellent pick-me-up for any tired plants, or as a boost to water seedlings or potted plants.

CAN I ADD TOO MUCH COMPOST?

Test the pH of your compost with a kit from a garden centre. Neutral pH is 7, anything below is acid (not enough lime), and anything above is alkaline (too much lime).

Healthy topsoil should be around 10 per cent organic matter. This may not sound very high but when you add well-rotted balanced compost to a receptive soil it gets incorporated without adding greatly to the overall percentage, so it is hard to add too much. But there are situations when you can get it wrong. It depends what your compost is made from, what your soil and climate is like, and what you intend to grow.

Balancing the diet

If you always use the same materials in your compost heap you can eventually overload the soil with some elements. If your compost is too nitrogen-rich you'll encourage sappy and leafy growth at the expense of rooting and fruiting. If you use too much fibrous material you could starve the soil of nitrogen.

If you are worried that you are adding too much of the same materials to your compost heap, you can always add some plants such as horsetail to vary the recipe (see pages 18-19).

Instead of buffering your soil's pH (see page 14) you can make your soil less hospitable – for example if you make very acidic compost. If you are composting large amounts of garden waste, and your soil tends to be rather acidic, your compost will be increasingly acidic so you must be sure to add lime to your heap.

If your soil needs regular liming, your compost heap will also need regular additions for balance. If your soil is (more rarely) too alkaline, you may need to add powdered gypsum or sulphur to your pile.

RESOURCES

Organisations to join
Centre for Alternative Technology (CAT)
Machynlleth
Powys SY20 9AZ
01654 702400
info@cat.org.uk

HDRA, the organic organisation
Ryton Gardens, Ryton on Dunsmore
Coventry
Warwickshire CV8 3LG
024 7630 3517
enquiry@hdra.org.uk

Soil Association
Bristol House, 40-56 Victoria Street
Bristol BS1 6BY
0117 929 0661
info@soilassociation.org

Suppliers
Chase Organics
Riverdene Business Park, Molesey Road
Horsham
Surrey KT12 4RG
01932 253666
www.OrganicCatalog.com
suppliers of seeds, tools and equipment

Blackwall Ltd
Seacroft Estate, Coal Road
Leeds LS14 2AQ
0113 201 8000
Suppliers of compost bins, including the
Blackwall Compost Tumbler (pictured page 53)

Gardening on the web
Centre for Alternative Technology (CAT)
www.cat.org.uk

HDRA, the organic organisation
www.hdra.org.uk

Organic UK
www.organic.mcmail.com

Soil Association
www.soilassociation.org

The Compost Resource Page
www.oldgrowth.org/compost

More books to read
Peter Harper, *Natural Garden Book*, Gaia
Books, 1994

Lawrence D. Hills, *Fertility Gardening*, David
and Charles, 1981

Organic Gardening magazine, *The Rodale
Book of Composting*, Rodale Press, 1992

Pauline Pears, *All About Compost*, Search
press/HDRA, 1999

John Seymour, *The Complete Book of Self
Sufficiency*, Dorling Kindersley, 1997

Sue Stickland, *The Small Ecological Garden*,
Search press/HDRA, 1996

INDEX

A GAIA ORIGINAL

Books from Gaia celebrate the vision of Gaia, the self-sustaining living Earth, and seek to help its readers live in greater personal and planetary harmony.

Design	Lucy Guenot, Mark Epton
Editor	Pip Morgan
Index	Mary Warren
Photography	Steve Teague except page 53, by Blackwall Ltd
Production	Lyn Kirby
Direction	Joss Pearson, Patrick Nugent

This is a Registered Trade Mark of Gaia Books Limited.

First published in the United Kingdom in 2001 by Gaia Books Ltd, 66 Charlotte Street, London W1T 4QE

ISBN 1 85675 117 1

A catalogue record of this book is available from the British Library.

Printed and bound in Italy

10 9 8 7 6 5 4 3 2

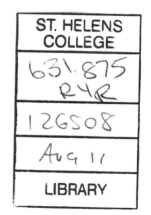

The Edible Container Garden

Michael Guerra ISBN 1 85675 089 2 £11.99
Plan well, plant properly and care for your soil for maximum produce from minimum space.

A Heritage of Flowers

Tovah Martin ISBN 1 85675 093 0 £14.99
This book tells of the history of old-fashioned flowers, both garden and wild, and the importance of their continued survival.

Heritage Vegetables

Sue Stickland ISBN 1 85675 033 7 £14.99
A guide to collecting, exchanging and cultivating old-fashioned vegetable seeds, and why you should choose to grow them.

The Gaia Natural Garden

Peter Harper ISBN 1856751732 £14.99
A beautiful guide to harmonizing gardening with the natural world. Foreword by Geoff Hamilton.

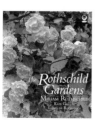

The Rothschild Gardens

Miriam Rothschild et al ISBN 1 85675 112 0 £16.99
Wildflower meadows, parks and gardens created by the Rothschilds. Photography by Andrew Lawson.

To order a book please phone: 01476 541 080 or fax: 01476 541 061
If you would like further details on Gaia titles please contact:
Gaia Books Ltd, 66 Charlotte Street, London, W1T 4QE
Tel: 020 7323 4010   Fax: 020 7323 0435
website: www.gaiabooks.co.uk